Becoming Accountable

Deryck Cheney

ISBN: 1503199452
ISBN 13: 9781503199453
Library of Congress Control Number: 2014920387
CreateSpace Independent Publishing Platform
North Charleston, South Carolina

A year from now, you will thank yourself for what you started today.
—**Deryck Cheney**

Contents

Preface

I was born a coach. I've enjoyed other roles, but I've always known this is who I am. I first realized this at the age of twelve, teaching my six-year-old brother how to play tennis. I was hooked—there was so much joy in watching someone learn and grow! I've always had a passion for business, too, because numbers and sales were things I understood well. In college, I double-majored in business and psychology to capitalize on these two strengths. Upon graduation, I set off on a career path that has led me to build a number of successful companies, along with forays into corporate America, and have eventually circled back to life coaching and building businesses. My achievement has been the marriage of my two skillsets—business acumen and psychology.

It's been an interesting path. The insights I've gained on my journey, through much trial and error, are what I hope to share in this book. Navigating transitions in my life and making the necessary changes hasn't always been easy, but I'm excited to share my process for creating and sustaining positive changes, so you can start living the life you were meant to live.

Are you someone who wants to actualize a dream you've contemplated for years, to improve in a difficult area, or simply to move your life in a more positive and fulfilling direction? Like me, you are a dynamic, unique human being, shaped, for better or for worse, by past experiences. You have your own skillsets, strengths, and personal challenges. I want to share with you how you can change your future, systematically and purposefully—that is what this book is all about. You do have the ability to create the life you've dreamed of! I am here to show you how.

You'll find that this book is not only about creating change in your life—it's also about sustaining that change. The following pages present an approach that empowers you to *consistently* implement changes and improve on your desired areas of growth. This is not just a theory—the book replicates an actual journey that has been successfully completed by others who have gone before you. I myself have used these techniques, and I feel confident they can work for you, too.

Early in my contemplation, I tried to learn everything I could about how to make changes in my life. During my free time, I would study best-selling coaching books and look at blogs and videos. I was always searching for a common theme—I wanted to completely understand. Was there a universal wisdom shared by the people who were helping others to change, grow, and become? A few key themes were becoming clear: I saw my successes were related to certain positive habits I'd developed, and I was building a solid list of behaviors and thinking patterns that had sustained me in challenging moments.

While I was studying all the greatest teachers, I realized I was tapping back into my inner coach. I would talk to anyone who seemed to be struggling with an issue, and I began working with people to help them get to where they wanted to be. It wasn't long before I faced a critical juncture in my own life: Should I stay with a great company that provided a fantastic income, or should I take a leap of faith and pursue life coaching? I decided to take the daring choice.

It was time to utilize all the knowledge I had acquired over the years. Interestingly, I'd always felt as if there was something missing in the programs I read about. This all changed when I experienced two major breakthroughs. My first breakthrough was the concept of "becoming accountable" for the positive life changes I was envisioning for myself. The second breakthrough was what I now refer to as "the happiness gap."

One day in a coffee shop I noticed a gentleman who had a fantastic energy. I went up to him, introduced myself, and explained my goals. After we had talked for a while, I asked if he'd be willing to become my weekly accountability partner. He was on board, right from the beginning. We agreed to videotape our sessions, so we could look back in a year's time to see what we had learned. I also called one of my best friends from college and extended the same invitation, which he accepted. What I learned over the course of that year is the basis of this book. Coaching through accountability is a foundational component of making the changes you want in your life. Please visit www.ctalife. com for upcoming events, audios, and videos regarding accountability in your own life.

The other concept that has been transformational in the coaching process is what I call "the happiness gap." A *gap* can be defined as a break in continuity or a space between two objects. When I refer to "the happiness gap," I want you to visualize the distance you perceive between where you are in life and where you hope to be. This book teaches you how to identify the happiness gap in your life and to bridge or close the gap. It's as simple as that. By following this process, you'll be living the life you know you were created for.

Change doesn't just magically happen, nor will simply reading this book get the job done. As with any great success story, personal transformation happens over time, through a combination of focus, persistence, resilience, and support. Together, we'll establish the skills and habits that will enable you to persist through setbacks, and we'll develop flexible, resilient thought patterns to keep you focused on your goals. Most importantly, you will find the support you need to make lasting changes that are congruent with your vision and purpose. You are the catalyst and fuel for this process—this book will give you the engine to harness your inner power.

Becoming Accountable begins with a process designed to reconnect you with yourself, examine your life, and identify the areas in which you need or want to make changes. You'll learn how to create value-based visions as a foundation for everything you do. Yet this foundational work is only the beginning of the process—and here is the uniqueness of this approach: we will use this powerful initial work to develop lasting activities and habits designed to propel you toward your vision. A principle of accountability completes the program, helping you stay on track to reach your visions.

Becoming Accountable is a process, and more importantly, a way of life. Be confident that you are on a path of discovery, growth, and positive change that will help you shape reality and actualize the inner dreams you have close to your heart.

To become what we are capable of becoming is the only end in life.
—Robert Louis Stevenson

Introduction

I could easily begin this book with a "What *Not* to Do" section. I'm here to tell you that there are many ways to go about the business of life all wrong. You probably have your own list of "strategies" that have left you off-balance and ready to try something new. In fact, a quick glance at contemporary America reveals that many people are suffering—you are not alone. Marriages continue to struggle. Many families live paycheck to paycheck. Obesity is an epidemic that even affects our children. Stress-related insomnia and depression top the charts for health issues that seem to be addressed primarily through prescription medications. The nightly news reminds us over and over just how challenged we have become as a society. We desperately need change and effective ways to stay on course.

Personally, I had gone about so many things the wrong way, striving for far-out goals that I thought would make me happy. In reality I was another casualty with a huge happiness gap, sleep issues, and stress far beyond what I could handle. As I searched for the answers, however, I stumbled upon the truth—happiness is not a mere destination. My happiness was found in the chase, in bridging the gap between my value-based visions and reality. This work has brought me the happiness I thought would always elude me, and I haven't even reached all of my goals yet!

Our founding fathers declared the pursuit of happiness an inalienable right. Unfortunately, our present culture spends billions trying to define happiness for us, while simultaneously convincing us that we don't have it! Most people spend their lives pursuing other people's definitions of happiness. Advertisers seek to make you feel less attractive, less valuable, and even less happy, so that you need to buy their products. Think about it—we receive the message "You aren't good enough" hundreds of times every day. The latest car ads chide us our car is old and needs servicing. Weight loss programs bombard us with reminders that we aren't models. The never ending release of electronics has heralded a notion of continual "upgrading." Our computers are even programmed to constantly stream advertisements tailored to our spending habits so we are never more than one click away from the next buy that could finally make us "happy."

Society defines success in terms of professional or financial achievement that enables conspicuous consumption. This whole system only works when we compare ourselves with someone else's ideas or standards, yet comparison is a trap most everyone falls into—over and over. For example, how often do we look at friends' recent Facebook pictures and find ourselves thinking, *Wow, they sure have great lives—mine isn't that good.*

To become truly happy, we must shut down these destructive voices and reconnect with our true selves. We must learn to listen to the sound of our own voices. As humans, we feel happy when we make progress toward our purposes, missions, and visions. There will never be a time when you instantly arrive at happiness—nor is it something way off in the distance. Does this sound like a paradox? It's not! This book will teach you my two key principles to live by: Happiness can be yours in the present, if you stay focused in your *pursuit* of it; and happiness can only be achieved when you've defined what it means to you. It has to be your definition—it can't be anyone else's. You will use the accountability program together with daily and weekly check-ins to continually come back to this key insight.

The first exercises in this book ignite the process of self-reflection and jog your memory of who you really are. Please give yourself plenty of time to delve into this process—it will be a great investment of your time and energy. The clearer you become about who you are, the easier it will be to define your vision. You'll also complete an evaluation to identify which areas of your life are strong points and which ones need more work. Most people find they are very strong in some areas of life, but not in others. Bringing your life into congruence with your value-based vision is the focus of closing the happiness gap, the space that is separating your values and visions from the reality of your life.

After analyzing your current life balance sheet and reconnecting to your true self, you will focus on writing your value-based vision statement. Your value-based vision will change your life—this exercise has the ability to transform everything. For example, if you value being a leader but find yourself in a job that offers no opportunities for leadership, you are going to experience a happiness gap. When our visions and reality don't match, it just doesn't feel right. You will have the chance, through this process, to either put yourself onto a path where your leadership skills will be utilized, or else to realign your vision with your current reality. Remember, life is always a series of events that either drives you closer to living your vision or further away. That is why we must consistently evaluate our visions and recalibrate our actions to stay on track.

Your value-based vision then becomes your lighthouse in the storm. You can orient all your decisions around this guiding principle. When you move toward your true self, things get easier for you. You wake up without an alarm, exercise, and eat well, because you *want* to have the best health—you want to live fully. You make your spiritual life a priority because you know this is vital to being the best you can be. You desire to read and learn because you naturally become more interested in improving. You want to grow as a parent, friend, or spouse—to develop as a great person to be in a relationship with. You engage in becoming the best that you can be, because that is *fun*!

I once heard a sermon about some little-known trivia. While many of us know that Roger Bannister was the first person to break the four-minute mile, not as many are familiar with the man who broke that record just six weeks later, John Landy. This sporting rivalry prompted a race between the two men, which would later become known as the "miracle mile." Millions watched this race—its ending moments are one of the most telling instructions we could find on how to win. As the gunshot signaled the start of the race, Landy ran ahead and set a torrid pace. He held that position all the way through the final turn. As the finish line came into view, John Landy was in the lead. No one knows why, but he slowed his pace a little and turned his head to look over his left shoulder, to see what was going on behind him. As he did this, Bannister was able to race by him on the right side, to win the race and take the title as the fastest man. Landy was worried about what was behind him, while Bannister focused on what was ahead.

This story illustrates why it's so important to move forward. You must dedicate yourself to a vision and focus your movement in that direction. If you stay pinned down by your past, or glorify what you once had, you aren't free to be in the present and to move in the direction you want to go. Imagine how Landy felt, looking over his shoulder, worried about what was coming—then think about how Bannister felt as he surged to the end and took the prize—you can see that happiness is truly found in the chase!

Good things come to those who wait, but the best things come to those who get up and go after them.
—Deryck Cheney

one

Reconnecting to Yourself

You are a unique creation of God, but do you really know what you were created for, or how to live comfortably as that person? This may sound like a cliché, but for many of us, it is true. We have forgotten who we are—we have lost the connection to our inner compass amid the daily stress and demands of our lives. This section presents a way to jump-start the self-reflection process and to refocus on the essential qualities and interests that make us unique beings.

I clearly remember sitting on the sidelines when my kids were taking their first tennis lessons. The coach had forgotten that my oldest son was a lefty. I watched as over and over the coach let my son struggle to hit the ball with his right hand. I was so frustrated and angry with that coach that I pulled my kids from the program. It was only later that I realized the real issue—I knew I would be the best coach for my kids, and I was sitting on the sidelines instead of embracing this opportunity I craved. While I continue to work with my kids, I have now found amazing coaches to help them reach their visions as well.

When you aren't connected to your true self, your life begins to drift off course. As you answer the following questions, take as much time as you need to really consider your answers, together with any feelings they may evoke. You will then use this momentum to examine the key areas of your life and uncover the core values from which your visions will spring. I also recommend checking out www.ctalife.com for "Unplugged" seminars and retreats designed to help you get the most out of this exercise, In the meantime, please do "unplug," make yourself comfortable, and enjoy this time with yourself.

What qualities do you value most in yourself?

_____

_____

_____

_____

_____

_____

List some compliments you frequently receive

_____

_____

_____

_____

_____

_____

What gives you the most joy in life?

_____

_____

_____

_____

_____

_____

If money were no object, how would you spend your life?

_____

_____

_____

_____

_____

_____

If you could change up to three things about yourself with a snap of the fingers, what would they be?

_____

_____

_____

_____

_____

_____

How would you like to spend the last years of your life?

_____

_____

_____

_____

_____

What do you want to try, explore, or accomplish that has been on your mind for some time?

_____

_____

_____

_____

_____

If you had more time in your day, how would you spend it?

_____

_____

_____

_____

_____

Do you have a motto or philosophy? If so, what is it?

_____

_____

_____

_____

_____

_____

What have you enjoyed accomplishing in your life?

_____

_____

_____

_____

_____

_____

When do you feel most alive or fully engaged in what you are doing?

_____

_____

_____

_____

_____

_____

What are some qualities you admire or are most attracted to among the significant people in your life?

_____

_____

_____

_____

_____

_____

What would you want people to say at your funeral?

_____

_____

_____

_____

_____

_____

Do you think others know the "real" you and would agree with most of your answers here? Why or why not? Does it matter to you?

_____

_____

_____

_____

_____

_____

Did you enjoy reconnecting with the many gifts and talents you have? Are there qualities you neglect to recognize in yourself on a day-to-day basis? Perhaps you're wondering how you've drifted so far from who you really are. Does your sense of the "real" you correspond with the person your friends know?

Come back to this exercise as often as you like to reconnect with the inner voice that speaks for the real you. God created you as a one of kind, and when you are living in congruence with this person you are most effective in following your value-based visions and closing the happiness gap.

It is never too late to be what you might have been.
—George Eliot

two

The Six Anchor Points of a Balanced Life

Now that you've reconnected with your true self, it's time to examine your current life and how reflective it is—or isn't—of that person. In this section we will delve into six key areas of life that we must maintain. To achieve your potential and to optimize the life you desire, you will need to establish balance among these areas. As with many things, when we are out of balance, our weak points overly stress our stronger ones. This imbalance creates chaos and strain. Likewise, if we focus too much of our attention on a single area, other areas fall into disorder. While finding balance is probably the most daunting challenge we face, a realistic, healthy, and quantifiable assessment will provide invaluable insight and direction. Before we begin the evaluation, let's take a closer look at the areas we will address and how they tie together in creating your vision.

First of all, you may ask, *why six?* You may argue there are countless ways to improve our lives; however, I've found that by distilling key concepts into six overarching categories, daily life becomes easier to manage. Close your eyes and visualize an anchor with three points on the top and three points on the bottom. This is a perfect image of a reliable support, firmly securing us to the right vision and purpose in our lives. Just as a broken anchor will set a ship adrift in a storm, so our lives are cast off course when our anchors are not firmly set and compatible with our values and visions. You will continually come back to these areas to review and restructure your activities and behaviors so that they remain congruent with your values. Through careful examination, you can always regain the momentum you need to power on toward your vision.

Your inner compass (spirituality). In this area, we explore the thoughts and behaviors associated with a strong, healthy spirituality and purpose (not specific religious beliefs or practices). The term *spirituality* here refers to a connection we have with something greater than ourselves. It can be the inner voice that makes us question, reflect, and remember that we aren't alone in this universe, and that, indeed, there is more to this life than waking up and making it through the day. As you develop your spirituality—whether you are starting with a blank slate, a deeply negative stance, or a vibrant faith life—you will see the path to your visions become both clearer and more attainable. There is a creator who already knows your destiny and is rooting for you to actualize all of your potential.

My own personal journey from occasional church attendance to a living, growing faith has been a game changer to say the least. For many years I didn't have much of a spiritual practice, I simply set a goal and went after it. Nine times out of ten, I would accomplish it. There came a time, though, when I realized there were far too many things in life I couldn't control. As I weighed all the pressures and demands of my life, they all seemed to be crashing in on me. When I became reliant on my faith, I saw at once that God had made me who I was, and I didn't have to try to be someone I wasn't. I began to give over many of my cares, worries, and stresses to Him. If you aren't sure where you stand on this matter, or perhaps even feel this isn't an area of your life you want to explore further, I encourage you to continue reflecting on what steps you might take for positive growth that is meaningful to you in this area.

Your outer connections to the world (relationships). We all want to be loved! At birth, we attach, preferably in a healthy way, to our primary caregivers. From that day forward, we are in a constant process of growth in this area. Our family dynamics, friendships, and romantic relationships are constantly evolving, and they are often a great source of both the joys and sorrows in life. As most of us have found, relationships don't come with an instruction manual. By their nature relationships always involve another person with his or her own unique personality traits, issues, and communication patterns. In this area, positive growth—in which your relationships are evolving in healthy ways—can reap so many benefits for both you and those you love. As you grow and mature in your personal relationships, you will find that other aspects of your life will make positive forward gains along with this area.

For many years, my wife and I would have long discussions that would never seem to resolve the issue we were debating. We read about the art of communication and how to talk about things that were difficult, but it took a wise person to point out that our deficit wasn't in our ability to communicate—our difficulty was in being able to *listen* to the other person. When I began to educate myself about active listening and reflecting my consideration, our relationship improved dramatically, and consequently so did most of the other important relationships in my life. I could communicate better with my children, coworkers, clients, and even my parents.

The captain of your ship (psychological well-being). Someone once told me that my thoughts created my feelings, which in turn created my behavior. This was truly a life changing moment! Our thinking has tremendous power—the old adage "You are what you eat" is just as applicable to our thoughts: "You are what you think." You can change your behaviors when you change the way you think about things, and consequently you can transform the emotions evoked from those thoughts.

I've always worked in sales, which is a very up-and-down business. Over the years, providing for my family has been both a blessing and a curse. We've been abundantly blessed, yes, but there have also been downturns when I had to be very mindful of our finances and where the next deal was going to come from. At these times, my feelings were reactive to my thoughts of worry and stress. I would struggle to remain positive and often lost sleep and the ability to be present with family and friends. I have learned to better manage my thoughts so that I remain effective, purposefully maintaining balance in my life. This can be one of the greatest challenges we face, as many of our thoughts are learned patterns in response to the varied experiences that shape us into the person we are. Learning to recognize thought patterns, both those that help and those that hinder us, is essential in reaching our vision and purpose.

What holds it all together (physical health). I have a Joel Osteen inspirational book in my bathroom that often catches my eye. I wonder if he realizes how distractingly white his teeth are! It seems impossible that he naturally looks the way he does, which gets me to thinking on how much time this person must spend on his appearance. Then I laugh at myself for how easily I am distracted from the purpose of the book, which is trusting in God to provide everything we need, and I have to redirect myself to my own goals and visions. The takeaway though, is that Joel seems super-successful, looks great, and probably takes good care of himself, but we can't know this for sure just based on his appearance. We also really don't need to look like Joel, or anyone else who might be the "picture" of success and good health. We must learn to listen to our inner voice that tells us when we aren't taking good care of ourselves. However, there is a fine line between our inner critic and the current American frenzy to be ageless and attractive. This can be a challenge to navigate, so we are going to explore some realistic, commonly agreed-upon health practices beneficial in providing the physical resources you need to reach your vision. The focus of this section is not on your appearance but your health.

Someone has to foot the bill (work/career/financial well-being). Money. It can be a blessing or a curse; it can make things happen or break things down, and there aren't many things that can compete with its ability to motivate, create, destroy, distract, or influence. Tied to this powerful force is our need to do something meaningful, to utilize our skills and talents, and to account for many hours of our time and energy. Money is one of the most-mentioned topics in the Bible, and there is no school in America where the mantra "What do you want to be when you grow up?" isn't a regularly discussed topic. There is no way around it—the management of our careers, finances, and resources is a powerful part of our life that we can't overlook. When this area of life is out of sync with our vision, we are fundamentally hindered in being the best we can be and often feel derailed from our dreams. Alternatively, when we optimize our skills and talents and purposefully live our lives, we can trust that we'll have what we need. We can earn and spend our money *on purpose*, not in reaction to the world we live in.

Fun! (taking time for your personal enjoyment and relaxation). Yes, I am including fun as a key area of a balanced life! When you were little, no one had to schedule your fun time. You played, and through play you learned, you enjoyed, and you were healthy. It is equally important for adults to schedule time for fun in their lives. Maintaining a hobby, friendships, and time for leisure are necessary for your heart, soul, and mind to be renewed.

As my responsibilities have grown through the years, it has become more and more important to be sure that I build in time to relax, laugh and step back from all the "work" of living. When you create time for fun in your life, you uphold your sense of self and provide an outlet for natural stress relief. You might need to work at this, or you might even be someone who needs to do a little less of this; however, having fun as part of your life is something that brings balance. It gives you a chance to experience happiness in the midst of work, resets your energy, and is good for your health!

Do not chase success, determine to become a person of value and then success will chase you.
—**Deryck Cheney**

three

Assessment Time!

So where do you stand? It's time to assess! Use the following scale from one to ten to gauge where you are currently functioning in these key areas of life.

Strongly Disagree	Disagree	Neutral	Agree	Strongly Agree
(0–1)	(2–3)	(4–6)	(7–8)	(9–10)

Spirituality

1. I practice my faith regularly. _____

2. I see the beauty in most everything and everyone. _____

3. I approach others with a loving attitude. _____

4. I live in the present, knowing my vision for the future. _____

5. I treat everyone as my equal. _____

6. I rarely judge people. _____

7. I routinely practice forgiveness with everyone in my life. _____

8. I am generous with my time, my money, and my energy. _____

9. I spend time learning about and focusing on my spirituality_____

10. I often use my spirituality to help solve problems. _____

Total: _____

Relationships

1. I have an inner circle of close friends. _____

2. All of my significant relationships are a positive influence on my life. _____

3. I am genuinely enthusiastic when something goes right for my spouse, children, or friends. _____

4. I have a sense of peace, joy, and security in my relationships. _____

5. I actively engage in learning how to be a better spouse, parent, or friend. _____

6. I say I love you regularly to those I love and try to show it with my actions. _____

7. I am willing to change in order to be a better parent, spouse, or friend. _____

8. I understand how to forgive, and I ask for forgiveness in my relationships. _____

9. I feel great about my relationships and actively work to improve them. _____

10. I know how to be assertive and can resolve
conflicts effectively. _____

Total _____

Psychological Well-Being

1. I'm not overcome by emotions or feelings of fear,
anger, love, guilt, jealousy, or worry. _____

2. I neither underestimate nor overestimate my abilities. _____

3. I have a tolerant, easygoing attitude toward
myself and others. _____

4. I can laugh at myself and accept my shortcomings. _____

5. I understand that my thoughts create my emotions. _____

6. I accept that I will have good days and bad days
as a part of life. _____

7. I feel as if I could handle almost any situation
that might arise. _____

8. I am resilient and flexible when responding
to change or stress. _____

9. I maintain a proactive approach toward potential problems. _____

10. I have effective coping strategies for stress and good
emotional support systems in place to work through
difficult situations. _____

Total _____

Physical Health

1. I do strength training three times a week.   _____

2. I do cardiovascular training that is appropriate for
   my age three times a week.   _____

3. I rarely eat fast food.   _____

4. I sleep a minimum of seven and a half hours nightly.   _____

5. I do not have any active addictions.   _____

6. I drink sixty-four ounces of water daily.   _____

7. I am at my ideal weight for my age.   _____

8. I eat a healthy balanced diet and take nutritional
   supplements as needed.   _____

9. I am happy with my health and generally feel well
   and energized.   _____

10. I visit the doctor and dentist regularly for checkups and
    follow all the recommended preventive care for my age. _____

                                          Total   _____

Work/Career/Financial Well-Being

1. I have a detailed budget, and I stick to it.   _____

2. I have a complete six-month reserve fund of all monthly
   expenses, and I have no credit-card debt.   _____

3. I understand there will be a time in my life when I no longer work—I have a detailed financial plan to prepare for that time. _____

4. My job provides the income that I need to support my family and manage my financial goals; it is appropriate compensation for the work I do. _____

5. My work utilizes my gifts and talents. _____

6. My family and I are fully and properly insured. _____

7. I regularly educate myself on best practices for personal finance management. _____

8. I am able to save and give generously on a regular basis. _____

9. I take vacations and focus on other areas of my life when not working. _____

10. I strive to be the best I can be in my chosen profession and regularly seek to improve my skills and productivity. _____

Total: _____

Fun!

1. I regularly spend time doing something I enjoy every week. _____

2. I look forward to leisure time and make plans to do fun activities. _____

3. I plan multiple vacations every year and "disconnect" for a majority of the time in order to relax and recharge. _____

4. I frequently find things to smile about and enjoy making others smile. _____

5. My close relationships are not negatively impacted by my leisure activities and are balanced with my other responsibilities. _____

6. I have fun and connect with others in my community outside of social media. _____

7. I look forward to downtime, when I can relax and spend time alone or with close friends. _____

8. I am able to laugh and joke around on a daily basis to help relieve stress. _____

9. As I finish leisure activities, I return to my responsibilities and other daily activities and routines without disappointment. _____

10. I am not using leisure activities to avoid my responsibilities or the steps I need to follow my vision. _____

Total _____

Now that you've completed your assessment, let's take a moment to reflect on the results. What do the numbers mean? Keep in mind that I've included some lofty aspirations on each listing. It's not likely that many of us will ever score 100 points in any of these key areas, but if you scored a total of 50 or below on any area, it is definitely time to take a closer look and work to achieve balance. As you move closer toward creating your value-based vision statement, you need to reflect on these areas and consider how they impact your ability to function at your best. Once you have formed your value-based vision and are closing your happiness gap, come back and retake this assessment. I think you'll be surprised by the personal growth that comes with living life on purpose!

What you do speaks so loudly that I cannot hear what you say.
—Ralph Waldo Emerson

four

Values: Determining Your Life through the Lens of Your Heart

We've all heard about values, but less about why it's important to identify our values and write them down. There are no guarantees in life, but I can say that when you are clear on your core values—the fundamental beliefs that color everything you do, think, and feel—your purpose becomes more focused. More importantly, when you establish your goals and vision with those values in mind, you will be astonished by the result. Your values are revealed in the forces that attract you—when you are living a value-based vision you will be propelled out of bed by those same forces.

For example, if you value physical fitness, you might be excited to do your exercise program and love to peruse blogs on healthy eating. If time with family is a core value for you, you'll probably jump out of bed on the first day of vacation in anticipation of time spent with those nearest and dearest to you. So the closer we can get our visions to match who we are at our core, the easier it will be to harness the motivation we'll need to create and sustain positive changes in our lives. Congruence between our values and vision is the most important part of the work we do in this book, as it is this work that helps to bridge the happiness gap. This correlation can single-handedly propel or derail our efforts.

To take another example, let's say you equally value being a provider and having fun. If your job—the primary method of providing for your family—isn't fun for you, you may soon find yourself very conflicted at work. You desperately want to be a provider, *but* can't stand being miserable in a job you don't like. Developing skills to change your career and transition to a position that provides both fun and a stable income would bridge the happiness gap and align your values and vision. In recognizing the interplay of our values with our visions, goals, and behaviors, we have the greatest potential to actualize the life we've always dreamed of.

When I speak of living with values at the core of what we do, I'm reminded of a great friend of mine, who is not only a mentor to me but also one of the best leaders I've ever known. We were roommates in our twenties when he got his first job—selling toilets. We sure had some laughs over the great investment his parents had made in his college education! Truly, though, he was completely focused on his vision, and his vision matched his values. He knew he wanted to be a leader and a provider for his family. He worked at developing himself, both professionally and personally, and is now a great leader in both his company and in his family.

He has risen through the ranks to achieve amazing things in his career. I'm sure he sold a lot of toilets in those early years, but that wasn't his focus. He always knew where he was heading, and those early sales goals were just a means to an end. Today he provides for his family and continually pursues growth in all areas of his life. It's all about the journey for him. The alignment of his values and visions are the key to his happiness. Incidentally, he is an accountability partner I meet with on a monthly basis. Value-based visions and accountability are a path you can confidently follow!

Your next step is to spend some time figuring out what *your* core values are. You may be surprised at the results, so this will be another great activity to set aside some time to really consider. The primary goal is to identify the six core values that are the *most* important to you. In the box below I've provided many words to give you a springboard into the activity. Perhaps you have another word that resonates with you more personally—please feel free to add it. I advise you to think carefully about every word below and how it might be applicable to your life.

Be aware of any associations or stigmas you might connect to certain words or traits. It can be challenging to choose a characteristic that you feel is perceived as unattractive or undesirable, even if your heart is calling it out as a core value. For example, if you grew up in a very hard-charging, competitive family, selecting *service* or *harmony* could provoke inner conflict. Nevertheless, if you desire harmony at your core but have placed yourself in an aggressively competitive workplace just to impress your family, you are likely to be miserable. You are much better off to come to terms with the incongruity and recognize if this could be a part of your happiness gap.

Read through this list a few times and add any words that come to mind during the process. Remember, your task is to select the six primary values that are the strongest motivators for you. Try to pull out the values that have the most impact in your life.

adventurous * risk-taker * thrill-seeker * speculative * daring * experimental * beautiful * creative * elegant * dependable * coach * encourager * influential * energetic * contributor * service * supportive * enthusiastic * strong * facilitator * minister * provider * designer * original * achievement * successful * caring * planner * builder * reliable * inspiring * leader * follower * loyal * friend * listener * committed * loyal * spiritual * peaceful * wealthy * funny * entertainer * showman * loving * athletic * community-oriented * family * natural * nurturer * inventor * intellectual * generous * competent * confident * fun * sensitive * optimistic * innovative * dreamer * empathetic * compassionate * honorable * accepting * patient * persistent * disciplined * passionate * religious * educated * teacher * prepared * consistent * uplifting * respected * accomplished * genuine * fulfilled * responsible * cheerful * collaborator * communicator * competitor * brave * daring * decisive * determined * diligent * effective * efficient * expressive * fair * friend * focused * forgiving * grateful * giving * frugal * happy * heroic * ingenious * humorous * peaceful * flexible * harmonious * hospitable * inspiring * independent * helpful * intuitive * investor * inventive * knowledgeable * kind * just * joyful * intense * innovative * imaginative * healthy * insightful * influential * humble * honest * intimate * resilient * logical * learner * open-minded * fun-loving * motivated * positive * respectful * fit * athletic * traditional * organized * thoughtful * lucky * be free* team-oriented * free-spirited * orderly * balanced * candid * confident * fearless * proactive * reactive * resourceful * reflective * respected * wise * unique * warm * thrifty * supportive * spunky * synergistic * timely * volunteer * sophisticated * reverent * satisfied * significant * self-reliant * poised * persuasive * perceptive * pragmatic * playful * nonconformist * entrepreneur * systematic * involved *gallant * ethical * dutiful

Now list these six words, and try to prioritize them—the first value being the most important to you.

    1. _____

    2. _____

    3. _____

    4. _____

5. _____

6. _____

If this exercise was a challenge for you, you are on the right track! Values compete fiercely with one another—the more we recognize how our values are at play, the more effective we can become at living our value-based vision. You may also discover that your actions and behaviors are not supported by your values—this is where our future work begins. You want to be living a life that reflects the values you hold most dear! Perhaps you are still not entirely sure what your core values are? The following exercise will help you to think deeply about your life, your values, and the way others perceive you.

Craft a sentence about yourself that includes the six words you selected. Read it to yourself a few times. Does it fit well, and do you get a jolt of excitement reading it? Are there other words you wanted to include or change? Keep working through this process until you do feel excited about the sentence. It should be a powerful declaration and speak to your heart.

Example (value words in italics). "I am a *faith*-centered *family* man and *provider* who *serves* others in a spirit of *fun* and *leadership*."

_____

_____

_____

_____

_____

_____

Congratulations! You just wrote your value-based vision statement!

Even if you're on the right track, you'll get run over if you just sit there.
—Will Rogers

five

Value-Based Visions

Now that you've seen the connection between your core values and their impact on the vision you have for yourself, it's important to understand the difference between a vision and a goal. Visions are very different from goals—goals generally represent concrete benchmarks that we can track and work toward. Losing weight, having a certain job or income level, visiting faraway places, or accomplishing a specific task, such as running a marathon, are all goals. Those are actually great goals, and they could be results of the work you are doing now; however, they are *not* visions. As you begin to craft your first round of visions—yes, you may draft multiple versions of your visions—you need to focus on who you are as a person and how that *feels*. Remember, your vision is your new day-to-day reality, not an end result!

To begin this process, you will create an overarching vision for yourself, such as the draft vision you just created, which will be supported by six particular visions based on the six anchor points of a balanced life. As you begin the accountability phase of the program, you will only focus your energy on one to three areas at a time; however, you will always keep your main vision at the forefront of your mind. Everything you think, do, and say should be congruent with your value-based vision. Try tackling some of the areas in which you scored lowest—after all, finding balance is the most important way you can free yourself to achieve your vision.

Keep in mind that your vision statement will be very succinct. Because it will say a lot in just a few words, those words must be very carefully chosen. The key to a good vision statement is to think in a long-term, broad sense, and be clear about who you are, as well as who you wish to become.

Let me give you a few examples:

"I touch the lives of many people, millions and millions, empowering them to achieve personal and career happiness and success."

"I am a leader in my organization, helping transform it into an organization that respects all its stakeholders—while at the same time being the best husband and father I can be."

My own personal vision is: "I am a *faith*-centered *family* man and *provider* who *serves* others in a spirit of *fun* and *leadership*."

As you craft your vision, you should incorporate your core values into the statement as you did in your practice in the previous chapter. Additionally, you will want to find an inspirational quote or Bible verse that inspires you to achieve your vision. It should provide personal affirmation that your vision and values are truly aligned. In the workbook portion of this book you will begin to select activities, routines, and behaviors to adopt as you begin your journey toward becoming your vision. You may also have habits, thoughts, or behaviors that you'll want to change or remove from your life. Every week you will have a chance to review your progress and redirect your actions and behaviors toward your value-based vision.

The Bible says, "Where there is no vision, the people perish" (King James Version). I think most of us can relate to the feeling of being lost and disconnected, essentially operating without a vision. However, there is an equally disastrous situation of creating a vision that isn't truly your own. I can't tell you how many times I've gone through this exercise, only to come away with someone else's vision! Here's the reason why: we get so much input from the significant people in our lives, and our world in general, that it is often challenging to discern our own vision from that of others. Our families, friends, and colleagues all have worthy aspirations—great-sounding goals that might make us better people, too—but this does not necessarily mean they are right for us.

In this process, you will find the support you need to write carefully crafted visions that are adaptable to *your own* life needs, wants, and challenges, and most importantly, congruent with who you are and who you want to be! You may be thinking, *How in the world do I get on the right path with my visions and not end up with a seemingly unattainable list of things to do and acquire? How is this any different from my last set of failed New Year's resolutions or crash diet?* This book's vision worksheets are designed to keep you focused on living out your vision every day.

The built-in accountability of weekly get-togethers will be the safeguard you need to achieve your vision of who you are meant to be. I can't recommend enough that you find an accountability partner, group, or coach to help you on this journey. I have individual, group, and live coaching programs available at www.ctalife.com that could be instrumental in helping you through this process. Our life circumstances and focus can fluctuate wildly, but with weekly accountability, you have the chance to make small changes and reorient yourself to your vision, creating the momentum to stay the course.

I became aware of the concept of "becoming" one weekend at a Cub Scouts camp in the woods with my son. As I sat by the fire, I realized that my visions needed to reflect the kind of person I wanted to be, not just the behaviors or material things I was adding to my life. The "who" was just as important as the "what." All my previous studies had focused on attaining specific goals as opposed to growing into the person I wanted to be, confident that my goals would be reached as a natural offshoot of the process. As I watched my son interact with his friends at the campsite, I saw that becoming who we were meant to be is the most important thing we can do. As my thoughts changed to incorporate this vision, my feelings, actions, and behaviors began to align naturally and work in unison. You will see this process becomes most effective when we train ourselves, through habits and accountability, to take proactive steps toward our vision.

You may want to fine-tune your vision as you progress and that's OK. Your vision will help you succeed far beyond where you'd be without one, because it is a clear extension of who you are at your core. That vision becomes a picture in your mind's eye that will serve as a lighthouse in the storm. We all know there are many detours and unexpected challenges that befall us, but if we keep clear visions that are in line with our core values, we will be able to navigate more successfully toward being the person of our value-based vision.

Are you ready to write? Hold those thoughts for just a moment more. The next two sections are closely tied to the vision process and provide a framework for how the whole program comes together.

For where your treasure is, there your heart will be also.
—Matthew 6:21

six

The Happiness Gap

Now it's time to really acknowledge where your happiness gaps are occurring. I've already touched on these incongruities as the source of many problems we experience in daily life. A happiness gap is a space that forms between our visions, our beliefs, and our *actual* lives. As you have begun to really focus in on your core values and how they might come together as a vision for your life, you might be feeling some angst that you are nowhere near your vision. Some of us are truly living with a Grand Canyon-size gap in our existence, while others may be doing well, with only a few areas that are slightly out of sync. Whatever the situation, when we aren't living according to our core values, there is a gap in our lives that makes happiness harder to access. I'm convinced that depression can stem from the helpless feeling many people face when the gap between their vision and their life seems insurmountable.

If you are a young person just starting out in life, it is important to become aware of your values so you can make corrections as you begin to navigate toward your vision. The job, friends, spouse, and lifestyle you choose will have a tremendous impact on your life! Choose wisely and be prepared to evaluate your decisions and make adjustments to stay on the right course. Those of us who have already set sail on a particular ship may realize it isn't headed in a direction that aligns with our values—we feel off course and even the happy moments in life lose their joy. While it is hard work to change direction, it's never too late! Let's evaluate our happiness gaps and learn some strategies for checking in with our goals and visions before we make decisions.

In order to see how closely your values and behaviors align, you need to examine the tangible elements of your life that "show" exactly what you are prioritizing. The most effective way to approach this exercise is to clear an afternoon to really sit down and consider where your time, money, and energy have been spent over the last few weeks. Yes, this takes effort, but there is nothing more concrete than examining the books. Time to work! Pull out your bank statements, e-mails, to-do lists and calendars, and take a close look. Calculate the five areas you spend the most time on in a week (excluding sleep), then tally up the top five expenditures in your life, and finally list the top three things that you think about in a week. Exactly where are you spending your time, money, and energy? Are these elements congruent with the values you listed in the core-value exercise? When you see the results, you can assess your own happiness gap and begin focusing your visions to narrow that gap.

Time

1. _____
2. _____
3. _____
4. _____
5. _____

Money

1. _____
2. _____
3. _____
4. _____
5. _____

Energy

1. _____
2. _____
3. _____
4. _____
5. _____

As you tally these elements do you see any surprises? Do you value being a family person but find that your children are fifth on the list? Do you value generosity yet notice that charitable giving or volunteer service are not among your priorities? We often fall into patterns and habits that are not really reflective of who we are or who we want to be.

When our time, resources, and energy are not being used congruently with our value-based visions, we are increasing the happiness gap. It is important to have all the different facets of our life in alignment and working together effectively. Perhaps you are wondering how to do all of this? Maintaining clear value-based visions and accountability are the keys to making the changes you desire and narrowing the happiness gap. I want you to return to this exercise in a year's time and walk away confident and secure that you are using your time, money, and energy in a way that is reflective of the real you!

I'm often asked to give an example of what a happiness gap might look like in real life. One of my accountability partners provides the perfect example to illustrate the concept. This friend is the most hardworking, conscientious father husband, and provider I know. The value he places on taking care of his family and being the best husband and father he can be are evident in everything he does. Not surprisingly, they are a pretty fantastic family with a lot of great things going for them. He has mentioned a number of times, though, that he feels guilty when he has a few drinks on the weekend and smokes the occasional cigarette. He doesn't do either of these activities to excess and is certainly not doing anything wrong or to expressly contradict his value-based vision. But there is enough of a discrepancy for it to fester and cause him discomfort.

This is a happiness gap. He will need to decide whether he wants to change his value-based vision to incorporate these activities as a way to relax from time to time, or whether he must modify his actions and behaviors (namely, stop drinking and smoking) to match a vision he has of a father who doesn't partake in these behaviors. Learning to isolate and examine our happiness gaps and readjust our visions or behaviors are skills we develop over time. There are many areas of dissonance we experience in the course of life. Recognizing the need to make adjustments can transform a sense of helplessness into an empowered and focused style of living. It will take time, but through weekly practice you *can* identify—and shrink—the happiness gaps in your life!

Don't you realize that in a race everyone runs, but only one person gets the prize? So run to win! All athletes are disciplined in their training. They do it to win a prize that will fade away, but we do it for an eternal prize. So I run with purpose in every step.
—1 Corinthians 9:24–26

seven

Do the Next Right Thing! Sustaining the Changes You Desire through Accountability

If you had everything you wanted in life and were wholly the person you were created to be, you would not still be reading this book. You have come so far—reconnecting to yourself, identifying your core values, getting ready to verbalize your visions—yet you're probably starting to realize that none of this means much if there aren't some real *changes* in your life.

We're all *great* at starting programs, easily rattling off a list of things we ought to change, and spending tons of mental energy wishing things could be different. We join gyms, start diets, get an idea for a business, or pick up the new self-help best seller, but that's where it ends. Does this happen because we are bad people? No, of course not! We want to change, grow, and improve; but, frankly, trying to make drastic changes without a plan leaves us exhausted, discouraged, and even further from our vision than when we started. And that is where this book is different. I've done the exact same thing, too many times to even tell! It was only through the process of recognizing a pattern, researching effective ways to change, and trial and error, that I've gotten to a place where I can confidently tell you change *can* happen!

Daily discipline and weekly accountability are not very glamorous ideas. You might feel a little stress just reading the words *daily* and *discipline* in the same sentence, but these are the game changers! We all want a magic wand that will magically transform our life. We do mental calisthenics to plan monumental life change. (Ever try and convince yourself that you'd consume only liquids for ten days to lose twenty pounds, or that you'd *never* yell at your kids again?) All we really need to do is take small steps, one day at a time. Consistency is the engine that will drive any change you want in your life—it is more transformational than anything I've ever encountered.

Through years of coaching tennis—from teaching my brother, to a tennis-coaching business I had in my twenties, to teaching my own young children—I have learned that from beginner to professional, the number one way to win any match is to be more consistent than your opponent. Make *fewer* errors (not none, just fewer)! Will making fewer errors get you on ESPN? Not likely, but a crazy one-in-a-thousand shot is sure to get some airtime! Being consistent, disciplined, and proactive are countercultural concepts. Just think of the million quick-fix programs out there and the instant gratification of Internet shopping and on-demand services. There is not a lot of encouragement to delay gratification and be disciplined. However, if you make this significant change in your thinking, you can have the one-in-a-million life you've always dreamed of.

You will need to build muscles to stay the course. This program is not designed to help you figure out your goals, it's designed to help you become the person you envision and to sustain the life changes, thoughts, and actions that reflect your vision. With practice you move to the next level and become proficient. Self-discipline helps you work the muscles you haven't used in a while and keeps you on track to sustain the momentum you are gathering.

I've always found that having a coach provides the encouragement, feedback, and motivation necessary to work through the pain of building new skills and muscles. I know my greatest growth has come when a coach or mentor helped me to stay the course and do what needed to be done to move to the next level. Coaching through accountability is the idea that a coach can hold you accountable to the standards you are setting for yourself. You won't always have great weeks, but if you find someone you can trust to keep you accountable to being the person of your vision, you will be well on your way to attaining balance. Simply put, accountability is a team effort. You will need to find a friend, group, or a coach to help you with this process. Feel free to ask special people in your life, those who have similar visions or determination, or visit my website, www.ctalife.com, to find out about private or group coaching.

Accountability is the insurance plan of this program—it ensures that even when the mood is gone, you will still have encouragement to bring that vision back to the forefront of your mind, to power on with the behaviors you'll need to make changes, and to document how far you've actually come! We are assured of two things in life: first, no one is perfect; and second, that we are all going to die. Know that you will face setbacks, need to adjust, be resilient, and persist—this is part of life. We all mess up and get off track, but I have factored this into my book from the beginning and plan to be there to help you adjust course and get back in motion. Accountability has a bad connotation for some people, particularly in our very independent culture, but one of the truly fun things in my life is being held to the standards I set for myself. It is so reassuring to know that even when I mess up, I can push the restart button every week.

Resilience is an object's ability to regain its original shape or function; just as a tree bends in the wind and then returns to its original shape, we need to build resilience in our lives. You must build enough resilience that when you are stretched and changed by circumstances, habits, and destructive thinking patterns, you can come back to your original shape and move forward as you were meant to. We all get blown off course, but the resilient regain their original focus and move ahead to the next great thing. Accountability helps us build resilience and persist when change is hard!

Vision statements are powerful, but along the journey we often find that we haven't quite centered on the right vision; or as we grow, change, and mature, our visions need to be more reflective of who we are in the process of becoming. Working in a weekly accountability group or with a coach, you can review your visions as well as behaviors and activities that you found either supported you or hindered you on your path. An accountability group or partner should help you focus on the *process* and not the product—you can't even begin to imagine the difference it will make in your life!

The following weekly worksheets are geared to reconnecting you to your vision, while also inspiring you to refine it, or to get back on track when you are derailed. They also remind you of just how far you have come! Fill in your sheet every Monday, and share it with your accountability group or partner; then check off your accomplishments each day, noting your victories, defeats, and miracle moments. (You know that awesome feeling when something goes so right you can hardly believe it's true!) Think of these accomplishments as the highlights of the past week. Then think of the "one thing" you want to accomplish in the upcoming week to move you closer to your vision. It's that easy!

Come back every Monday to recharge, with your group or coach, and reconnect to the person of your vision! Don't forget to flip back to the activity bank for ideas on things to add or subtract every week. Finally, don't forget the old adage, "How do you eat an elephant? One bite at a time."

Courage doesn't always roar. Sometimes courage is the little voice at the end of the day that says "I'll try again tomorrow".
—**Mary Anne Radmacher**

Appendix A: Vision Worksheets

Spiritual Vision:

_____

_____

_____

_____

My core value that matches this vision is:

_____

My Bible verse or inspirational quote that affirms my vision is:

_____

_____

_____

_____

The thoughts, activities, routines, and behaviors I will need to be doing on a daily basis to achieve this are:

- ☐ _____
- ☐ _____
- ☐ _____
- ☐ _____
- ☐ _____

The routines/habits that I will need to stop doing on a daily basis are:

- ☐ _____
- ☐ _____
- ☐ _____
- ☐ _____
- ☐ _____

Relationship Vision:

_____

_____

_____

_____

My core value that matches this vision is:

_____

My Bible verse or inspirational quote that affirms my vision is:

_____

_____

_____

_____

The thoughts, activities, routines, and behaviors I will need to be doing on a daily basis to achieve this are:

- ☐ _____
- ☐ _____
- ☐ _____
- ☐ _____
- ☐ _____

The routines/habits that I will need to stop doing on a daily basis are:

- ☐ _____
- ☐ _____
- ☐ _____
- ☐ _____
- ☐ _____

Psychological Vision:

_____

_____

_____

_____

My core value that matches this vision is:

_____

My Bible verse or inspirational quote that affirms my vision is:

_____

_____

_____

_____

The activities, routines, and behaviors I will need to be doing on a daily basis to achieve this are:

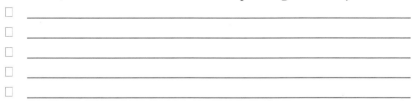

- ☐ _____
- ☐ _____
- ☐ _____
- ☐ _____
- ☐ _____

The routines/habits that I will need to stop doing on a daily basis are:

- ☐ _____
- ☐ _____
- ☐ _____
- ☐ _____
- ☐ _____

Physical Vision:

_____

_____

_____

_____

My core value that matches this vision is:

_____

My Bible verse or inspirational quote that affirms my vision is:

_____

_____

_____

_____

The activities, routines, and behaviors I will need to be doing on a daily basis to achieve this are:

- ☐ _____
- ☐ _____
- ☐ _____
- ☐ _____
- ☐ _____

The routines/habits that I will need to stop doing on a daily basis are:

- ☐ _____
- ☐ _____
- ☐ _____
- ☐ _____
- ☐ _____

Work/Career/Financial Vision:

_____

_____

_____

_____

My core value that matches this vision is:

_____

My Bible verse or inspirational quote that affirms my vision is:

_____

_____

_____

_____

The thoughts, activities, routines, and behaviors I will need to be doing on a daily basis to achieve this are:

- ☐ _____
- ☐ _____
- ☐ _____
- ☐ _____
- ☐ _____

The routines/habits that I will need to stop doing on a daily basis are:

- ☐ _____
- ☐ _____
- ☐ _____
- ☐ _____
- ☐ _____

My Fun Vision:

_____

_____

_____

_____

My core value that matches this vision is:

_____

My Bible verse or inspirational quote that affirms my vision is:

The thoughts, activities, routines, and behaviors I will need to be doing on a daily basis to achieve this are:

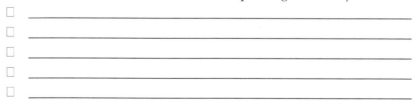

The routines/habits that I will need to stop doing on a daily basis are:

☐ _____
☐ _____
☐ _____
☐ _____
☐ _____

The greatest glory in living lies not in never fall-ing, but in rising every time we fall.
—Nelson Mandela

Appendix B:

Weekly Accountability Worksheets

MY VALUE-BASED VISION

BIBLE VERSE/INSPIRATIONAL QUOTE

VICTORY:

_____

_____

_____

DEFEAT:

_____

_____

_____

MIRACLE MOMENT:

_____

_____

_____

ONE THING:

_____

_____

_____

DAILY DISCIPLINE SCHEDULE

Monday:_____

Tuesday:_____

Wednesday:_____

Thursday:_____

Friday:_____

Saturday:_____

Sunday:_____

MY VALUE-BASED VISION

BIBLE VERSE/INSPIRATIONAL QUOTE

VICTORY:

_____

_____

_____

DEFEAT:

_____

_____

_____

MIRACLE MOMENT:

_____

_____

_____

ONE THING:

_____

_____

_____

DAILY DISCIPLINE SCHEDULE

Monday:_____

Tuesday:_____

Wednesday:_____

Thursday:_____

Friday:_____

Saturday:_____

Sunday:_____

MY VALUE-BASED VISION

BIBLE VERSE/INSPIRATIONAL QUOTE

VICTORY:

_____

_____

_____

DEFEAT:

_____

_____

_____

MIRACLE MOMENT:

_____

_____

_____

ONE THING:

_____

_____

_____

DAILY DISCIPLINE SCHEDULE

Monday:_____

Tuesday:_____

Wednesday:_____

Thursday:_____

Friday:_____

Saturday:_____

Sunday:_____

MY VALUE-BASED VISION

BIBLE VERSE/INSPIRATIONAL QUOTE

VICTORY:

_____

_____

_____

DEFEAT:

_____

_____

_____

MIRACLE MOMENT:

_____

_____

_____

ONE THING:

_____

_____

_____

DAILY DISCIPLINE SCHEDULE

Monday:_____

Tuesday:_____

Wednesday:_____

Thursday:_____

Friday:_____

Saturday:_____

Sunday:_____

MY VALUE-BASED VISION

BIBLE VERSE/INSPIRATIONAL QUOTE

VICTORY:

_____

_____

_____

DEFEAT:

_____

_____

_____

MIRACLE MOMENT:

_____

_____

_____

ONE THING:

_____

_____

_____

DAILY DISCIPLINE SCHEDULE

Monday:_____

Tuesday:_____

Wednesday:_____

Thursday:_____

Friday:_____

Saturday:_____

Sunday:_____

MY VALUE-BASED VISION

BIBLE VERSE/INSPIRATIONAL QUOTE

VICTORY:
_____
_____
_____

DEFEAT:
_____
_____
_____

MIRACLE MOMENT:
_____
_____
_____

ONE THING:
_____
_____
_____

DAILY DISCIPLINE SCHEDULE

Monday:_____

Tuesday:_____

Wednesday:_____

Thursday:_____

Friday:_____

Saturday:_____

Sunday:_____

MY VALUE-BASED VISION

BIBLE VERSE/INSPIRATIONAL QUOTE

VICTORY:

_____

_____

_____

DEFEAT:

_____

_____

_____

MIRACLE MOMENT:

_____

_____

_____

ONE THING:

_____

_____

_____

DAILY DISCIPLINE SCHEDULE

Monday:_____

Tuesday:_____

Wednesday:_____

Thursday:_____

Friday:_____

Saturday:_____

Sunday:_____

<u>MY VALUE-BASED VISION</u>

<u>BIBLE VERSE/INSPIRATIONAL QUOTE</u>

VICTORY:

_____

_____

_____

DEFEAT:

_____

_____

_____

MIRACLE MOMENT:

_____

_____

_____

ONE THING:

_____

_____

_____

DAILY DISCIPLINE SCHEDULE

Monday:_____

Tuesday:_____

Wednesday:_____

Thursday:_____

Friday:_____

Saturday:_____

Sunday:_____

<u>MY VALUE-BASED VISION</u>

<u>BIBLE VERSE/INSPIRATIONAL QUOTE</u>

VICTORY:

_____

_____

_____

DEFEAT:

_____

_____

_____

MIRACLE MOMENT:

_____

_____

_____

ONE THING:

_____

_____

_____

DAILY DISCIPLINE SCHEDULE

Monday:_____

Tuesday:_____

Wednesday:_____

Thursday:_____

Friday:_____

Saturday:_____

Sunday:_____

MY VALUE-BASED VISION

BIBLE VERSE/INSPIRATIONAL QUOTE

VICTORY:

_____

_____

_____

DEFEAT:

_____

_____

_____

MIRACLE MOMENT:

_____

_____

_____

ONE THING:

_____

_____

_____

DAILY DISCIPLINE SCHEDULE

Monday:_____

Tuesday:_____

Wednesday:_____

Thursday:_____

Friday:_____

Saturday:_____

Sunday:_____

MY VALUE-BASED VISION

BIBLE VERSE/INSPIRATIONAL QUOTE

VICTORY:

_____

_____

_____

DEFEAT:

_____

_____

_____

MIRACLE MOMENT:

_____

_____

_____

ONE THING:

_____

_____

_____

DAILY DISCIPLINE SCHEDULE

Monday:_____

Tuesday:_____

Wednesday:_____

Thursday:_____

Friday:_____

Saturday:_____

Sunday:_____

MY VALUE-BASED VISION

BIBLE VERSE/INSPIRATIONAL QUOTE

VICTORY:

_____

_____

_____

DEFEAT:

_____

_____

_____

MIRACLE MOMENT:

_____

_____

_____

ONE THING:

_____

_____

_____

DAILY DISCIPLINE SCHEDULE

Monday:_____

Tuesday:_____

Wednesday:_____

Thursday:_____

Friday:_____

Saturday:_____

Sunday:_____

MY VALUE-BASED VISION

BIBLE VERSE/INSPIRATIONAL QUOTE

VICTORY:

_____

_____

_____

DEFEAT:

_____

_____

_____

MIRACLE MOMENT:

_____

_____

_____

ONE THING:

_____

_____

_____

DAILY DISCIPLINE SCHEDULE

Monday:_____

Tuesday:_____

Wednesday:_____

Thursday:_____

Friday:_____

Saturday:_____

Sunday:_____

MY VALUE-BASED VISION

BIBLE VERSE/INSPIRATIONAL QUOTE

VICTORY:

_____

_____

_____

DEFEAT:

_____

_____

_____

MIRACLE MOMENT:

_____

_____

_____

ONE THING:

_____

_____

_____

DAILY DISCIPLINE SCHEDULE

Monday:_____

Tuesday:_____

Wednesday:_____

Thursday:_____

Friday:_____

Saturday:_____

Sunday:_____

MY VALUE-BASED VISION

_____

BIBLE VERSE/INSPIRATIONAL QUOTE

_____

VICTORY:
_____
_____
_____

DEFEAT:
_____
_____
_____

MIRACLE MOMENT:
_____
_____
_____

ONE THING:
_____
_____
_____

DAILY DISCIPLINE SCHEDULE

Monday:_____

Tuesday:_____

Wednesday:_____

Thursday:_____

Friday:_____

Saturday:_____

Sunday:_____

<u>MY VALUE-BASED VISION</u>

<u>BIBLE VERSE/INSPIRATIONAL QUOTE</u>

VICTORY:

_____

_____

_____

DEFEAT:

_____

_____

_____

MIRACLE MOMENT:

_____

_____

_____

ONE THING:

_____

_____

_____

DAILY DISCIPLINE SCHEDULE

Monday:_____

Tuesday:_____

Wednesday:_____

Thursday:_____

Friday:_____

Saturday:_____

Sunday:_____

<u>MY VALUE-BASED VISION</u>

_____

<u>BIBLE VERSE/INSPIRATIONAL QUOTE</u>

_____

VICTORY:
_____
_____
_____

DEFEAT:
_____
_____
_____

MIRACLE MOMENT:
_____
_____
_____

ONE THING:
_____
_____
_____

DAILY DISCIPLINE SCHEDULE

Monday:_____

Tuesday:_____

Wednesday:_____

Thursday:_____

Friday:_____

Saturday:_____

Sunday:_____

MY VALUE-BASED VISION

BIBLE VERSE/INSPIRATIONAL QUOTE

VICTORY:

_____

_____

_____

DEFEAT:

_____

_____

_____

MIRACLE MOMENT:

_____

_____

_____

ONE THING:

_____

_____

_____

DAILY DISCIPLINE SCHEDULE

Monday:_____

Tuesday:_____

Wednesday:_____

Thursday:_____

Friday:_____

Saturday:_____

Sunday:_____

MY VALUE-BASED VISION

BIBLE VERSE/INSPIRATIONAL QUOTE

VICTORY:
_____
_____
_____

DEFEAT:
_____
_____
_____

MIRACLE MOMENT:
_____
_____
_____

ONE THING:
_____
_____
_____

DAILY DISCIPLINE SCHEDULE

Monday:_____

Tuesday:_____

Wednesday:_____

Thursday:_____

Friday:_____

Saturday:_____

Sunday:_____

MY VALUE-BASED VISION

BIBLE VERSE/INSPIRATIONAL QUOTE

VICTORY:

_____

_____

_____

DEFEAT:

_____

_____

_____

MIRACLE MOMENT:

_____

_____

_____

ONE THING:

_____

_____

_____

DAILY DISCIPLINE SCHEDULE

Monday:_____

Tuesday:_____

Wednesday:_____

Thursday:_____

Friday:_____

Saturday:_____

Sunday:_____

<u>MY VALUE-BASED VISION</u>

_____

<u>BIBLE VERSE/INSPIRATIONAL QUOTE</u>

_____

VICTORY:

_____
_____
_____

DEFEAT:

_____
_____
_____

MIRACLE MOMENT:

_____
_____
_____

ONE THING:

_____
_____
_____

DAILY DISCIPLINE SCHEDULE

Monday:_____

Tuesday:_____

Wednesday:_____

Thursday:_____

Friday:_____

Saturday:_____

Sunday:_____

MY VALUE-BASED VISION

BIBLE VERSE/INSPIRATIONAL QUOTE

VICTORY:

_____

_____

_____

DEFEAT:

_____

_____

_____

MIRACLE MOMENT:

_____

_____

_____

ONE THING:

_____

_____

_____

DAILY DISCIPLINE SCHEDULE

Monday:_____

Tuesday:_____

Wednesday:_____

Thursday:_____

Friday:_____

Saturday:_____

Sunday:_____

MY VALUE-BASED VISION

BIBLE VERSE/INSPIRATIONAL QUOTE

VICTORY:

_____
_____
_____

DEFEAT:

_____
_____
_____

MIRACLE MOMENT:

_____
_____
_____

ONE THING:

_____
_____
_____

DAILY DISCIPLINE SCHEDULE

Monday:_____

Tuesday:_____

Wednesday:_____

Thursday:_____

Friday:_____

Saturday:_____

Sunday:_____

MY VALUE-BASED VISION

BIBLE VERSE/INSPIRATIONAL QUOTE

VICTORY:

_____

_____

_____

DEFEAT:

_____

_____

_____

MIRACLE MOMENT:

_____

_____

_____

ONE THING:

_____

_____

_____

DAILY DISCIPLINE SCHEDULE

Monday:_____

Tuesday:_____

Wednesday:_____

Thursday:_____

Friday:_____

Saturday:_____

Sunday:_____

MY VALUE-BASED VISION

BIBLE VERSE/INSPIRATIONAL QUOTE

VICTORY:

_____

_____

_____

DEFEAT:

_____

_____

_____

MIRACLE MOMENT:

_____

_____

_____

ONE THING:

_____

_____

_____

DAILY DISCIPLINE SCHEDULE

Monday:_____

Tuesday:_____

Wednesday:_____

Thursday:_____

Friday:_____

Saturday:_____

Sunday:_____

MY VALUE-BASED VISION

BIBLE VERSE/INSPIRATIONAL QUOTE

_____

VICTORY:

_____
_____
_____

DEFEAT:

_____
_____
_____

MIRACLE MOMENT:

_____
_____
_____

ONE THING:

_____
_____
_____

DAILY DISCIPLINE SCHEDULE

Monday:_____

Tuesday:_____

Wednesday:_____

Thursday:_____

Friday:_____

Saturday:_____

Sunday:_____

MY VALUE-BASED VISION

_____

BIBLE VERSE/INSPIRATIONAL QUOTE

_____

VICTORY:

_____

_____

_____

DEFEAT:

_____

_____

_____

MIRACLE MOMENT:

_____

_____

_____

ONE THING:

_____

_____

_____

DAILY DISCIPLINE SCHEDULE

Monday:_____

Tuesday:_____

Wednesday:_____

Thursday:_____

Friday:_____

Saturday:_____

Sunday:_____

MY VALUE-BASED VISION

BIBLE VERSE/INSPIRATIONAL QUOTE

VICTORY:

_____

_____

_____

DEFEAT:

_____

_____

_____

MIRACLE MOMENT:

_____

_____

_____

ONE THING:

_____

_____

_____

DAILY DISCIPLINE SCHEDULE

Monday:_____

Tuesday:_____

Wednesday:_____

Thursday:_____

Friday:_____

Saturday:_____

Sunday:_____

MY VALUE-BASED VISION

BIBLE VERSE/INSPIRATIONAL QUOTE

VICTORY:

_____

_____

_____

DEFEAT:

_____

_____

_____

MIRACLE MOMENT:

_____

_____

_____

ONE THING:

_____

_____

_____

DAILY DISCIPLINE SCHEDULE

Monday:_____

Tuesday:_____

Wednesday:_____

Thursday:_____

Friday:_____

Saturday:_____

Sunday:_____

MY VALUE-BASED VISION

BIBLE VERSE/INSPIRATIONAL QUOTE

VICTORY:
_____
_____
_____

DEFEAT:
_____
_____
_____

MIRACLE MOMENT:
_____
_____
_____

ONE THING:
_____
_____
_____

DAILY DISCIPLINE SCHEDULE

Monday:_____

Tuesday:_____

Wednesday:_____

Thursday:_____

Friday:_____

Saturday:_____

Sunday:_____

MY VALUE-BASED VISION

BIBLE VERSE/INSPIRATIONAL QUOTE

VICTORY:
_____
_____
_____

DEFEAT:
_____
_____
_____

MIRACLE MOMENT:
_____
_____
_____

ONE THING:
_____
_____
_____

DAILY DISCIPLINE SCHEDULE

Monday:_____

Tuesday:_____

Wednesday:_____

Thursday:_____

Friday:_____

Saturday:_____

Sunday:_____

MY VALUE-BASED VISION

BIBLE VERSE/INSPIRATIONAL QUOTE

VICTORY:

_____

_____

_____

DEFEAT:

_____

_____

_____

MIRACLE MOMENT:

_____

_____

_____

ONE THING:

_____

_____

_____

DAILY DISCIPLINE SCHEDULE

Monday:_____

Tuesday:_____

Wednesday:_____

Thursday:_____

Friday:_____

Saturday:_____

Sunday:_____

MY VALUE-BASED VISION

_____

BIBLE VERSE/INSPIRATIONAL QUOTE

_____

VICTORY:

_____

_____

_____

DEFEAT:

_____

_____

_____

MIRACLE MOMENT:

_____

_____

_____

ONE THING:

_____

_____

_____

DAILY DISCIPLINE SCHEDULE

Monday:_____

Tuesday:_____

Wednesday:_____

Thursday:_____

Friday:_____

Saturday:_____

Sunday:_____

MY VALUE-BASED VISION

BIBLE VERSE/INSPIRATIONAL QUOTE

VICTORY:

_____

_____

_____

DEFEAT:

_____

_____

_____

MIRACLE MOMENT:

_____

_____

_____

ONE THING:

_____

_____

_____

DAILY DISCIPLINE SCHEDULE

Monday:_____

Tuesday:_____

Wednesday:_____

Thursday:_____

Friday:_____

Saturday:_____

Sunday:_____

MY VALUE-BASED VISION

BIBLE VERSE/INSPIRATIONAL QUOTE

VICTORY:
_____
_____
_____

DEFEAT:
_____
_____
_____

MIRACLE MOMENT:
_____
_____
_____

ONE THING:
_____
_____
_____

DAILY DISCIPLINE SCHEDULE

Monday:_____

Tuesday:_____

Wednesday:_____

Thursday:_____

Friday:_____

Saturday:_____

Sunday:_____

MY VALUE-BASED VISION

BIBLE VERSE/INSPIRATIONAL QUOTE

VICTORY:

_____

_____

_____

DEFEAT:

_____

_____

_____

MIRACLE MOMENT:

_____

_____

_____

ONE THING:

_____

_____

_____

DAILY DISCIPLINE SCHEDULE

Monday:_____

Tuesday:_____

Wednesday:_____

Thursday:_____

Friday:_____

Saturday:_____

Sunday:_____

MY VALUE-BASED VISION

BIBLE VERSE/INSPIRATIONAL QUOTE

VICTORY:
_____
_____
_____

DEFEAT:
_____
_____
_____

MIRACLE MOMENT:
_____
_____
_____

ONE THING:
_____
_____
_____

DAILY DISCIPLINE SCHEDULE

Monday:_____

Tuesday:_____

Wednesday:_____

Thursday:_____

Friday:_____

Saturday:_____

Sunday:_____

MY VALUE-BASED VISION

BIBLE VERSE/INSPIRATIONAL QUOTE

VICTORY:

_____

_____

_____

DEFEAT:

_____

_____

_____

MIRACLE MOMENT:

_____

_____

_____

ONE THING:

_____

_____

_____

DAILY DISCIPLINE SCHEDULE

Monday:_____

Tuesday:_____

Wednesday:_____

Thursday:_____

Friday:_____

Saturday:_____

Sunday:_____

<u>MY VALUE-BASED VISION</u>

_____

<u>BIBLE VERSE/INSPIRATIONAL QUOTE</u>

_____

VICTORY:
_____
_____
_____

DEFEAT:
_____
_____
_____

MIRACLE MOMENT:
_____
_____
_____

ONE THING:
_____
_____
_____

DAILY DISCIPLINE SCHEDULE

Monday:_____

Tuesday:_____

Wednesday:_____

Thursday:_____

Friday:_____

Saturday:_____

Sunday:_____

MY VALUE-BASED VISION

BIBLE VERSE/INSPIRATIONAL QUOTE

VICTORY:

_____

_____

_____

DEFEAT:

_____

_____

_____

MIRACLE MOMENT:

_____

_____

_____

ONE THING:

_____

_____

_____

DAILY DISCIPLINE SCHEDULE

Monday:_____

Tuesday:_____

Wednesday:_____

Thursday:_____

Friday:_____

Saturday:_____

Sunday:_____

MY VALUE-BASED VISION

BIBLE VERSE/INSPIRATIONAL QUOTE

VICTORY:

_____

_____

_____

DEFEAT:

_____

_____

_____

MIRACLE MOMENT:

_____

_____

_____

ONE THING:

_____

_____

_____

DAILY DISCIPLINE SCHEDULE

Monday:_____

Tuesday:_____

Wednesday:_____

Thursday:_____

Friday:_____

Saturday:_____

Sunday:_____

MY VALUE-BASED VISION

BIBLE VERSE/INSPIRATIONAL QUOTE

VICTORY:

_____

_____

_____

DEFEAT:

_____

_____

_____

MIRACLE MOMENT:

_____

_____

_____

ONE THING:

_____

_____

_____

DAILY DISCIPLINE SCHEDULE

Monday:_____

Tuesday:_____

Wednesday:_____

Thursday:_____

Friday:_____

Saturday:_____

Sunday:_____

MY VALUE-BASED VISION

_____

BIBLE VERSE/INSPIRATIONAL QUOTE

_____

VICTORY:

_____
_____
_____

DEFEAT:

_____
_____
_____

MIRACLE MOMENT:

_____
_____
_____

ONE THING:

_____
_____
_____

DAILY DISCIPLINE SCHEDULE

Monday:_____

Tuesday:_____

Wednesday:_____

Thursday:_____

Friday:_____

Saturday:_____

Sunday:_____

MY VALUE-BASED VISION

BIBLE VERSE/INSPIRATIONAL QUOTE

VICTORY:

_____

_____

_____

DEFEAT:

_____

_____

_____

MIRACLE MOMENT:

_____

_____

_____

ONE THING:

_____

_____

_____

DAILY DISCIPLINE SCHEDULE

Monday:_____

Tuesday:_____

Wednesday:_____

Thursday:_____

Friday:_____

Saturday:_____

Sunday:_____

MY VALUE-BASED VISION

_____

BIBLE VERSE/INSPIRATIONAL QUOTE

_____

VICTORY:

_____
_____
_____

DEFEAT:

_____
_____
_____

MIRACLE MOMENT:

_____
_____
_____

ONE THING:

_____
_____
_____

DAILY DISCIPLINE SCHEDULE

Monday:_____

Tuesday:_____

Wednesday:_____

Thursday:_____

Friday:_____

Saturday:_____

Sunday:_____

<u>MY VALUE-BASED VISION</u>

<u>BIBLE VERSE/INSPIRATIONAL QUOTE</u>

VICTORY:

_____

_____

_____

DEFEAT:

_____

_____

_____

MIRACLE MOMENT:

_____

_____

_____

ONE THING:

_____

_____

_____

DAILY DISCIPLINE SCHEDULE

Monday:_____

Tuesday:_____

Wednesday:_____

Thursday:_____

Friday:_____

Saturday:_____

Sunday:_____

MY VALUE-BASED VISION

_____

BIBLE VERSE/INSPIRATIONAL QUOTE

_____

VICTORY:
_____
_____
_____

DEFEAT:
_____
_____
_____

MIRACLE MOMENT:
_____
_____
_____

ONE THING:
_____
_____
_____

DAILY DISCIPLINE SCHEDULE

Monday:_____

Tuesday:_____

Wednesday:_____

Thursday:_____

Friday:_____

Saturday:_____

Sunday:_____

MY VALUE-BASED VISION

BIBLE VERSE/INSPIRATIONAL QUOTE

VICTORY:

_____

_____

_____

DEFEAT:

_____

_____

_____

MIRACLE MOMENT:

_____

_____

_____

ONE THING:

_____

_____

_____

DAILY DISCIPLINE SCHEDULE

Monday:_____

Tuesday:_____

Wednesday:_____

Thursday:_____

Friday:_____

Saturday:_____

Sunday:_____

MY VALUE-BASED VISION

_____

BIBLE VERSE/INSPIRATIONAL QUOTE

_____

VICTORY:

_____
_____
_____

DEFEAT:

_____
_____
_____

MIRACLE MOMENT:

_____
_____
_____

ONE THING:

_____
_____
_____

DAILY DISCIPLINE SCHEDULE

Monday:_____

Tuesday:_____

Wednesday:_____

Thursday:_____

Friday:_____

Saturday:_____

Sunday:_____

MY VALUE-BASED VISION

BIBLE VERSE/INSPIRATIONAL QUOTE

VICTORY:

_____

_____

_____

DEFEAT:

_____

_____

_____

MIRACLE MOMENT:

_____

_____

_____

ONE THING:

_____

_____

_____

DAILY DISCIPLINE SCHEDULE

Monday:_____

Tuesday:_____

Wednesday:_____

Thursday:_____

Friday:_____

Saturday:_____

Sunday:_____

MY VALUE-BASED VISION

BIBLE VERSE/INSPIRATIONAL QUOTE

VICTORY:

_____
_____
_____

DEFEAT:

_____
_____
_____

MIRACLE MOMENT:

_____
_____
_____

ONE THING:

_____
_____
_____

DAILY DISCIPLINE SCHEDULE

Monday:_____

Tuesday:_____

Wednesday:_____

Thursday:_____

Friday:_____

Saturday:_____

Sunday:_____

MY VALUE-BASED VISION

BIBLE VERSE/INSPIRATIONAL QUOTE

VICTORY:

_____

_____

_____

DEFEAT:

_____

_____

_____

MIRACLE MOMENT:

_____

_____

_____

ONE THING:

_____

_____

_____

DAILY DISCIPLINE SCHEDULE

Monday:_____

Tuesday:_____

Wednesday:_____

Thursday:_____

Friday:_____

Saturday:_____

Sunday:_____

MY VALUE-BASED VISION

BIBLE VERSE/INSPIRATIONAL QUOTE

VICTORY:

_____
_____
_____

DEFEAT:

_____
_____
_____

MIRACLE MOMENT:

_____
_____
_____

ONE THING:

_____
_____
_____

DAILY DISCIPLINE SCHEDULE

Monday:_____

Tuesday:_____

Wednesday:_____

Thursday:_____

Friday:_____

Saturday:_____

Sunday:_____

Appendix C: Activity Bank

This supplement includes a list of positive endeavors to jump-start your daily practice, together with a section of negative mind patterns and activities to limit or avoid. Start with simple changes you feel confident you can implement. Build your momentum slowly and steadily. As you begin to see changes and are comfortable with your progress, slowly add tougher activities. Always come back to your visions to be sure you are making changes that will support you and add value to your life!

Spiritual Activities

- o Read a proverb every day.
- o Learn something new about your faith daily.
- o Offer spiritual encouragement to someone who made a difference in your life.
- o Read a daily devotional book.
- o Be involved in a small faith-based group
- o Pray or meditate.
- o Read the Bible or a spiritual guide.
- o Memorize Scripture.
- o Listen to faith-based music (or faith-based podcasts, sermons, etc.) while in the car, at home, exercising, etc.
- o Practice spiritual disciplines (i.e., silence, fasting, tithing, etc.).
- o Give praise and affirmation to others.
- o At the end of the day, write out what you are grateful for.
- o Think of others first.
- o Follow the Golden Rule (Do unto others as you would have them do unto you).
- o Take time to make someone else smile or feel good each day.

o   Say a blessing before meals.

o   Every evening, reflect on where you have met God during that day.

Relationship Builders

o   Eat dinner together as a family—everyone shares their best moment of the day.

o   Make a date night with your spouse, or plan a time with close family or friends.

o   Spend thirty minutes a day with your spouse.

o   Ask someone out on a date.

o   Have someone over for dinner and cook for him or her, no matter how bad a cook you are.

o   Speak well of your spouse in public.

o   Tell your spouse what he or she does well—be specific.

o   Tell someone you love why you appreciate him or her.

o   Make it clear to your spouse that he or she makes you happy.

o   Leave a message stating that you love your spouse.

o   Put your arm around your spouse in public.

o   Practice forgiveness with those you are close to.

o   Every night before bed, tell your children that you love them.

o   Once a month, take your child out to spend one-on-one time.

o   Be present at your children's events.

o   Encourage those around you, especially those you work with, or spend a lot of time with.

o   Make sure you talk to those you care about and that all communication is not done via electronics.

o   Be present in conversations.

o   Be flexible and tolerant of the challenges in your relationships.

o   Make the people you care about a priority in your life.

Physical Health Builders

o   Meditate for twenty minutes a day.

o   See a nutritionist, or read about healthy eating.

o   Schedule doctor exams and dental appointments regularly.

o   Reduce your sugar and caffeine intake.

o   Wake up at the same time every day.

o   Stretch for ten minutes a day.

o   Walk for thirty minutes a day.
o   Do strength training.
o   Do twenty minutes of cardiovascular exercise three times a week.
o   Drink a green smoothie.
o   Learn yoga or Pilates.
o   Eat breakfast.
o   Take the stairs.
o   Get seven hours of sleep.
o   Wear sunscreen.
o   Work in your garden.
o   Get a pedometer.
o   Have a "walking meeting."
o   Take a multivitamin or recommended supplements.
o   Floss your teeth daily.
o   Get preventive health care that is recommended by your physician.
o   Eat plenty of fruits and vegetables.

Psychological Health Builders

o   See a counselor to work through emotional wounds.
o   Meditate two times a day.
o   Listen to instructional audio in car.
o   Go to seminars.
o   Get a therapist or accountability partner.
o   Hire a coach.
o   Join a support group.
o   Smile at five people a day.
o   Reconnect with old friends.
o   Make new friends.
o   Commit to a new challenge.
o   Surround yourself with beauty.
o   Acknowledge your anxieties and fears.
o   Practice continual learning.
o   Watch inspirational videos.
o   Keep a journal.
o   Read a book on cognitive flexibility and resilience.

Career/Work/Financial Health Builders

- o   Keep a detailed spending diary for two weeks.
- o   Read Dave Ramsey's *Financial Peace.*
- o   Pay off loans and debts.
- o   Get term life insurance if you have dependents.
- o   Pay off debt the smart way: pay your highest-interest-rate loans first, then pay the next-highest debt, and so forth, until complete.
- o   Start contributing to an IRA.
- o   Build an emergency fund with an automatic savings plan.
- o   Stop renting and buy a home.
- o   Seek a meaningful job to challenge yourself.
- o   Learn to "time block" and manage your time effectively.
- o   Be diligent and dependable.
- o   Learn to ask for what you want.
- o   Network within your field.
- o   Make professional development a regular practice.
- o   Work hard when you are working; rest when you are not.
- o   If you aren't happy in your current career field, take an aptitude test and consider the results.
- o   Volunteer in the field that you want to work in.
- o   Concentrate on your strengths.
- o   Be on time or early for appointments.
- o   Dress appropriately for the work you do.
- o   Seek wise counsel for your finances and career aspirations.

There is only so much anyone can do in one day, but there are many things that we'd do well to reduce or eliminate! Here are some areas to limit or avoid.

Relationships Pitfalls

- o   gossip
- o   excess social media time
- o   saying yes to things that are not a priority for your visions
- o   yelling

o criticizing
o being in a bad mood
o pessimism
o holding a grudge
o not apologizing
o keeping secrets
o trying to "fix" the people you care about
o passive-aggressive behavior
o ingratitude

Physical Land Mines

o eating excessive sugar or carbohydrates
o excess caffeine
o fast food
o gluten
o white flour
o fatty foods
o smoking
o having more than one alcoholic drink a day
o habitually taking any pills that are addictive
o drugs
o soda
o skipping breakfast
o overtraining
o eating packaged foods
o sedentary practices (excessive TV, movies, computer time, etc.)
o texting or distracted driving

Spiritual Drains

o selfish behavior
o yelling or unjust anger
o cursing or negative language
o obsessively watching the news or reading negative materials
o bragging or boasting
o jealousy (coveting others relationships, possessions, etc.)

- o prideful behavior
- o continually worrying or being anxious over things you can't change or control
- o worrying about what others think
- o excluding others
- o judging others

Psychological Weapons of Mass Destruction

- o being uncontrollably or unjustifiably angry
- o cursing or negative language
- o complaining
- o reading gossip magazines
- o worrying excessively
- o bragging
- o isolating yourself
- o anxiety
- o criticizing
- o dwelling on failures
- o basing your self-worth on what other people think of you
- o jealousy or indulging in unhealthy comparisons with others
- o pessimism
- o watching TV in the bedroom
- o checking e-mail first thing in the morning
- o letting your past define you
- o being unaware of the relationship between your thoughts, feeling, and actions
- o blaming others
- o not accepting personal responsibility for your life and actions

Career/Work/Financial Saboteurs

- o any kind of wasteful spending
- o distractions
- o being lazy
- o blaming the government
- o blaming the economy

o   procrastinating

o   making excuses

o   giving up on your dreams

o   victim mentality

o   being afraid of failure

o   avoiding hard work

o   concentrating on your weaknesses

o   not learning how to manage your own finances

o   debt

o   not staying current in your field of work

Appendix D:

Inspirational Thoughts and Bible Verses

-Stop trying to be good at everything. Commit to being great at something you love.

-Own Monday mornings and you will own your life.

-Success is measured by what you do today.

-No matter how you feel, do the next right thing.

-Live according to *your* visions and values, not someone else's.

-Let go of the past, express gratitude for what you have, and look fervently to the future.

-There is a price to be paid for being yourself, but it's worth it.

-There is no substitute for hard work. There is nothing that cures anxiety more effectively than hard work.

-Surround yourself with people that see and honor your greatness.

-Success that comes quickly is actually luck.

-Learn to make your visions wild and exciting and your goals boring and specific.

-Practice honoring and tolerating differences with others on a daily basis.

-If you aren't excited about your visions, get new visions.

-Life isn't fair, don't quit, become resilient and ask yourself what you can do right now.

-Find ways to communicate truth in kind and gentle ways.

-Being bad at something is the first step to being really good at something. Be bad at something today.

For the spirit God gave us does not make us timid, but gives us power, love, and self-discipline.
—2 Timothy 1:7

Not only so, but we also glory in our sufferings, because we know that suffering produces perseverance; perseverance, character; and character, hope. And hope does not put us to shame, because God's love has been poured out into our hearts through the Holy Spirit, who has been given to us.
—Romans 5:3–5

Peace I leave with you; my peace I give you. I do not give to you as the world gives. Do not let your hearts be troubled and do not be afraid.
—John 14.27

"For I know the plans I have for you," declares the Lord, "plans to prosper you and not harm you, plans to give you hope and a future."
—Jeremiah 29:11

No temptation has overtaken you except what is common to man. And God is faithful; he will not let you be tempted beyond what you can bear, but when you are tempted he will also provide a way out, so that you can endure it.
—1 Corinthians 10:13

Be strong and courageous. Do not be afraid or terrified because of them, for the Lord your God goes with you; he will never leave you nor forsake you.
—Deuteronomy 31:6

Whatever your hand finds to do, do it with all your might.
—Ecclesiastes 9:10

I can do all this through Him who gives me strength.
—Philippians 4:13

Do not be anxious about anything, but in every situation, by prayer and petition, with thanksgiving, present your requests to God.
—Philippians 4:6

No discipline seems pleasant at the time, but painful. Later on, however, it produces a harvest of righteousness and peace for those who have been trained by it.
—Hebrews 12:11

Acknowledgments

I am grateful to many people who contributed to my life, my story, and this book.

First and foremost I am grateful to God, who has faithfully brought me through many storms. My family is next to thank for their love, support, guidance, encouragement, and the foundation they have provided. Specifically, I want to thank my wife, Elizabeth Cheney—thank you for sharing this life with me. I love you. My parents, Gordon and Victoria Cheney, and the rest of my family, who have always been there for me: Todd Cheney, the Bartlett family, the Roslewicz's, and Tom Roslewicz. I love you all. Gram and Jackie, you all are not only loved and loving, you have been an inspiration.

I have countless friends who have been significant in my journey. Garland and Shenley Williams—you are two of the best people on earth. I could write a whole book on the impact you have made in our lives. Russ Harris—my Friday accountability partner. Thank you for always being there. Dave Paccassi—my Monday morning accountability partner. Thank you for being loud that day in Panera. Mark Simpson—thank you for your help at a time most needed. It won't be forgotten. Kevin McGovern—what a blessing it was to call you "Coach." And Bryan Degabrielle—you are my lifelong best friend.

Tim Macgowan—thank you for bringing me to my faith and being a phenomenal mentor to me. Steve Jacobson—it was an amazing experience to get to watch you in action for five years. Laura Macgowan—thanks for your help on this. You have a bright future ahead of you as a writer.

I also wish to thank the following people whose friendship and support were invaluable: Kim Grim, Ben Chenault, Todd Gavinski, Arin Dibello, Paul Clements, Jose Soler-Baillo, Robert Klemish, Shaleeka, Alicia, Mark, Andrew, Gino, Thomas, Ed, Isaac Hull, Jonathan Schrag, Sean and Jill Doran, Louise Thaxton, Phil Shannon, Eric, Courtney, Kim the nurse, Dr. Weiner, Tim, Amit Kaim, Justin Exner, Melissa Okrasinski, Dave Gallegos, David Lazowski, Laura and Joey Reale, Eduard and Aida Frimel, Ricky and Kim Brown, Kristen and Bob Pegg, Bernice Holmes Minor, Michael Russell and the Wednesday Bible Group leaders and mentors at Fairway: Cindy, Ray, Steve Probst, and Paul Walnick.

And I thank you, dear readers. It is the countless faces I see in my mind's eye that inspired me to write this book and to create accountability and coaching programs that could be accessible to many.

Made in the USA
San Bernardino, CA
29 January 2015